CYBER LOVE

ANURADHA SRIVASTAVA

Contents

Prologue

Terms and Conditions

The Publisher has strived to be as accurate and complete as possible in the creation of this report, notwithstanding the fact that he does not warrant or represent at any time that the contents within are accurate due to the rapidly changing nature of the Internet.

While all attempts have been made to verify information provided in this publication, the Publisher assumes no responsibility for errors, omissions, or contrary interpretation of the subject matter herein. Any perceived slights of specific persons, peoples, or organizations are unintentional.

In practical advice books, like anything else in life, there are no guarantees of income made. Readers are cautioned to reply on their own judgment about their individual circumstances to act accordingly.

This book is not intended for use as a source of legal, business, accounting or financial advice. All readers are advised to seek services of competent professionals in legal, business, accounting and finance fields.

You are encouraged to print this book for easy reading.

Table Of Contents

Foreword

For many different reasons either personal or professional, many people are turning to online dating to find a partner. Although these reasons may vary greatly, all have the same goal in mind, and that is to find someone without having to go through too much time and hassle. Get all the info you need here.

Cyber Love

Chapter 1:

The benefits of finding your date online

Synopsis

The following are some of the benefits of finding a date through the online platform:

The Basics

Touted to be a safer way of finding a date, this is becoming a very popular platform sought after both by the male and female customer base.

The protection and privacy element it promises, until both parties are ready to actually make contact, is an attractive feature for those who are looking for a hassle free venture.

The cost tagged to this style of introductions is also comparatively cheaper that actually having to meet a person on an actual date before deciding their suitability.

Most of these online dating services only charge between $20 -

$50 for the membership fee, for which the member is then privy to profiles and photos of everyone listed.

The feature of being able to make contact based on the individual's won schedule is another attractive feature as there are no time restrictions because these sites are usually permanently open.

It also eliminates the need to put up with chance meetings and being able to match with people on the similar schedule base can be a good start.

Getting to know the other party without actually getting too serious or getting in too deep before any real decisions are made for physical contact is a feature that most members fine beneficial.

This way there are no unexpected problems arising from expectations from both parties, to complicate the connections made. Avoiding further contact with encountering individuals who seem too clingy can be done with this type of connection.

Chapter 2:

How online dating site works

Synopsis

There are a lot of complications and stages that are required in the game of dating today. Perhaps the most exhausting and time consuming phase of dating, lies in the initial stages where the meeting and elimination game is played.

With the introduction of the online dating sites some of these stages can be effectively handled and shortened to a certain extent, thus making the whole process easier, less stressful and certainly less time and energy consuming.

The following are some points as to how the online dating sites actually work:

How It Works

Once a site is chosen, the first step the individual would have to do would be to design and send in a profile of themselves. This profile should ideally include important information such as photos, age, occupation, hobbies, expectations and any other information the individual is willing to divulge that would enhance the chance of attracting interest from others.

The profile should also include a light and short and maybe even humorous essay style content of topics that interest the individual.

The next step would be to view other profiles and decide on the one that interest the individual. When these have been identified, then the individual would have to make the initial contact, by sending a short and hopefully interested and engaging message that will encourage the other party to respond positively.

Sometimes the site operators will match suitable candidates accordingly and notify the participants so that some contact can be made where there is interest.

After the corresponding stage the interested parties can take it a step further and actually plan a physical contact in the form of a date. This is usually done when both parties are comfortable enough to feel safe, thus the willingness to facilitate physical contact.

Chapter 3:

Finding the best dating sites

Synopsis

Because of the increasing popularity of this sort of service, there are so many different sites available on the internet, and this can be rather overwhelming and confusing.

Being already pressed for time and perhaps even being too exhausted to going through the more conventional dating motion the individual may decide to seek the services of a reputable dating site.

The following are some points that will help the individual to discern and pick the best sites instead of having to waste precious time and energy surfing sites randomly:.

The Best Sites

Finding a site that provides membership on a monthly basis usually be better than the one off payment sites. This is because these membership monthly charging sites are well designed and are more professionally run. Such sites will be very careful in vetting the members and their accompanying profile. The sites are also kept updated always and sometimes even help in prompting connections that maybe otherwise overlooked by the member.

A site that caters to the more serious individual, who is actually interested in finding a suitable partner, is better than sites that are just there for people to meet each other. The sites for the more serious intention members will have the added benefit of the site organizers actually matching suitable profiles with the hopeful intention of helping its member find partners quickly, effectively and efficiently.

If the individual have very specific requirements such as to do with religion or special interest and food categories, then using sites that cater for such niche groups is better that simply signing up randomly at just any dating site. There are several different dating sites and cater specifically to niche markets and it would be time and energy efficient to enroll in such sites.

Sites that have proven track records and provide statistical documentation, to back these claims is also a good choice to enroll into.

Chapter 4:

Easy steps to choose the right dating sites

Synopsis

Selecting a suitable dating site can be quite challenging, simple due to the fact that there are so many sites available on the internet. There are almost daily addictions and for the time constraints individual surfing through every site is simply not a viable option.

The following are some easy steps to follow when choosing a suitable dating site:

Some Tips

Deciding on the sites that would best suit the style and intention of the individual, is the first decision to make. There are some sites set up for the purpose of simple introducing and meeting other people with similar intentions.

These intentions may include just widening their existing friendship circles, making friends with like minded interests, meeting new and interesting people and other non serious committing liaisons.

Then there are site that are set up to specifically match people who are interested in finding partner to embark on serious relationships with the eventual of marriage in mind.

The next step would be to identify only active sites where the members are constantly or at least frequently visiting the site and even where there is a good amount of new members.

There should be clear indications of when members check the mail or even when they are online. This would effectively show the activity level the site is creating, thus giving the potential member an idea of its relevance.

The time frame aspect of the intended membership would also be something to be considered. Being prepare to sign up for a period

of more than 6 months would be ideal. The financial commitment should also be considered, if the time frame for the intended membership is going to be for at least 6 months. It should work out to be a cost effective commitment, when measure by the possible encounters promised.

Chapter 5:

Save time with online dating reviews

Synopsis

Using online dating services today can be quite a chore in itself, due to the fact that there is an overwhelming amount of such services being offered on the internet at any given time.

Therefore having the necessary information to help narrow down the search for the ideal site to use would be very helpful to the individual.

The following are some tips of how to identify online dating sites through the reviews provided:

Review Sites

As the review are basically designed to help the prospective client save precious time and money the usual elements to include would be getting the best deal and money's worth out of the sign up. The reviews here would provide the individual with the information about the detailed different levels of commitment in the membership fees and if the said fee is worth the services being provided. The services provided would effectively have to justify the cost demanded by the online dating service and the review would be able to shed light on this very important matter.

Another informative feature the reviews are able to provide is on the number of members available at the various sites and the amount of activity at the site. Having a lot of member but no real activity will not help the prospective client and may even be a waste of time, money and effort; therefore the reviews would ideally be able to provide information on these.

Review provided on certain specific features such as the demographics of a particular site would also be useful information to a prospective client. This would help the individual who is only interested in a niche area, thus relieving the individual from signing up at sites that would not be of any use to him or her.

Chapter 6:

Free membership dating sites

Synopsis

There is a lot of free membership dating sites on the internet today and understating what they are really all about will help the prospective client decide if this style of sites is suitable for their intended use.

Free dating sites are usually filled with members who are not really extremely serious about finding and making the one commitment to a lasting partnership.

Most of the members sign up at these sites just to "try" their luck, while others sign up to make new friends and form interesting liaisons, but the expectations are usually nominal and this makes the site very wide based and lack any form of discrimination.

<u>"Everything you want is out there waiting for you to ask. Everything you want also wants you. But you have to take action to get it."</u>

Free Sites

Free membership sites usually don't have very stringent policies in place and thus the protection feature is not really a prominently expected or required aspect of the sign up exercise. In this case the member will not be assured that the information provided is honest and trustworthy. There is very little tracking done to ensure all members have legitimate intentions for possible connections with others.

Most free dating site are rife the pop up advertisement and emails. This can be a very annoying interruption for the time and internet access restricted individual. Being bothered by such interruptions that don't really have any connection to the dating service is not only annoying, but is also time consuming to have to keep clicking them close. A lot of scammers feature their wares on this type of sites and sometimes this eventually affects the credibility of the sites.

Some free sites only accept members from certain parts of the world or from certain social standings. However there is very little verification exercises that are conducted to ensure those who sign up as members are actually following the requirements completely. Therefore although the site has certain rules and stipulations there is no guarantee that all the members conform to these prerequisites.

Chapter 7:

Paid membership dating sites

Synopsis

It is a common preconception that when something cost money it is usually better in quality and value when compared to something that is given away for free. The same can be said for the online dating sites as a whole, although there are some free sites that are quite good, but these are few and far between.

The following are some points that will show the benefits of choosing a paid membership site for dating services:

Paid Sites

The quality of the people who would consider signing up at paid membership sites is usually comparatively higher than other style sites. People who are willing to pay for services are typically more serious about the exercise of making genuine connection with others and are also from a better demographics platform.

The element of trust is arguably higher for those who sign up at paid membership sites. The general view is that, people who pay for something are perhaps more likely to be committed, thus availing themselves to actually making connections as much as possible. These members would take the time to design proper profiles, answer questions, and fill out forms and any other exercises that would be required at such dating sites.

In almost all such paid dating sites, the support and customer services given are of a better quality. The personnel at these sites are usually very committed to providing the services touted in their advertising campaigns. This is mainly due to the fact that such sites depend on the recommendations of satisfied existing members to broaden the revenue base, by introducing the site to others.

Most paid membership dating sites will be consistent in matching the members as frequently as possible. This matching will usually be done with the utmost care, as the members depend very much on the discretion of the service provider.

Chapter 8:

How to write an attractive profile

Synopsis

Being part of an online dating data base can be a very competitive platform to be part of. Therefore the individual would need to be able to present a very comprehensive and attention grabbing profile that would ensure the interest of other parties enrolled.

The following are some tips on how to prepare the ideal attention grabbing profile and will ensure huge amounts of interest:

Your Profile

Choosing a suitable user name would be the first step that is required of the new member. However some care should be taken when choosing this user name as silly and overly descriptive names are usually not encouraged or well received. Such choices would not help to convey the member's seriousness or commitment levels, in the venture at all.

Personal information should not be easily divulged, as there should be some level of privacy to ensure the member is adequately protected from unnecessary solicitation outside the safety of the online site. Giving out too much personal information, will only create a level of vulnerability that could endanger the member.

Including photos that are complimenting yet honest is another feature that is important to be included in a profile. Sad as it may seem, people are interested in knowing of the physical appearance of those they intend to communicate with before they decide to take the connection to the next level. Therefore if the member decides not to include any photos, the chances of getting any interested a "hits" would definitely be few and far between.

"Promoting" one's self online is also another feature that the member should be savvy in doing. This self promotion is what is going to get the individual noticed over the many others available at the site. This will also help to ensure the member stays competitive and relevant.

Chapter 9:

Finding partner with the same religion

Synopsis

Of late there are quite a few online dating services that cater to niche groups. This is getting to be a rather popular requirement especially when it comes to the topic or religious platform.

Many people today find it better and certainly less cumbersome in the long run, to be matched to potential partners that share the same religion.

Therefore making the effort to sign up at dating sites which specifically cater to the religious requirements of the member would be a better choice to make.

The Spiritual Side

Most people looking to make a connection on the dating site for eventually finding a life partner with the same religion would require for the site to have such a vetting platform in place. A religious based dating site would almost always encourage only members from that particular niche to sign on. Very rarely would they welcome someone who is not of the particular religious requirement or background, unless the said individual is completely open to eventually following the religious beliefs and practices of the party they choose to start a relationship with.

The spiritual and moral values of those who are serious about their faith is often a non compromising element that is insisted upon and diligently practiced. Thus it would be a complete waste of time to invest in the other party if there is no religious compatibility. Here the online dating service would play a very important role in ensuring only those suitable candidates are introduced to the members.

This convenience help all parties concerned to stay focused on other matter and eliminate the possible heart aches that could surface if there is no religious compatibility.

Because there are certain requirements that are practiced within the spectrum of the religion, being a member of a dating site that is designed to accommodate only these requirements would be a relief and welcomed service to the individual seeking such provisions.

Wrapping Up

As in everything there are always some bad individuals who come off as "rotten apples" and spoil everything for the rest of the generally honest and committed set of individuals. The same is true for the online dating scammers who rarely have good intentions in mind and are usually only looking to scam those they can.

The following are some areas to look into and be weary of when it comes to trying to avoid scammers for online dating:

It would be normal to assume some level of common sense, to be exercised and extended, when initiating contact with other members through the online dating platform. However in a lot of cases where scam have been reported, the common factor that seems to facilitate the scam is usually the lack of common sense.

There is nothing wrong in being weary and exercising caution when it comes to giving out personal information to virtual strangers when the connections are made at the dating sites.

Making sure not to be "sucked" in by seemingly honest individual is something that should be strictly adhered to as these scammers can be very convincing in their seemingly genuine presentations.

These scammers are almost always easily identifiable for those who are focused on being careful and weary of being duped. Most scammer will appear to be very interested and anxious to set up a physical meeting.

They would be constantly trying to get the other party to commit to setting up a proper date. Besides this, most scammer are very well schooled in the art of getting personal information from their targets. Therefore under no circumstances should the individual give out any information that can be eventually linked to them, especially if the eventual online connection does not work out as first desired.

<u>"Your whole life is a manifestation of the thoughts that go on in your head."</u>

DATING DO'S AND DONT'S

Terms and Conditions

The Publisher has strived to be as accurate and complete as possible in the creation of this report, notwithstanding the fact that he does not warrant or represent at any time that the contents within are accurate due to the rapidly changing nature of the Internet.

While all attempts have been made to verify information provided in this publication, the Publisher assumes no responsibility for errors, omissions, or contrary interpretation of the subject matter herein. Any perceived slights of specific persons, peoples, or organizations are unintentional.

In practical advice books, like anything else in life, there are no guarantees of income made. Readers are cautioned to reply on their own judgment about their individual circumstances to act accordingly.

This book is not intended for use as a source of legal, business, accounting or financial advice. All readers are advised to seek services of competent professionals in legal, business, accounting and finance fields.

You are encouraged to print this book for easy reading.

Table Of Contents

Foreword

Salvation in a little book, Dating Dos and Don'ts: A Single's Rulebook to an explosive love life is your ticket to Speed dating 101! If you're on a speed date, you're bombarded with a gigantic amount of personal info within a very short period of time.

This may be a bit overpowering, particularly when you're assessing which individual you'd like to see again, as well as startling, since you'd want to be on your toes to impress, but your dates are all up in your face.

Not to worry though, with this marvelous little book, you've got a wingman and life and love guru all in one! Get all the info you need here.

Dating Do's And
Don'ts - The Singles Rulebook An Explosive Love life

Chapter 1:

Introduction

Synopsis

As you only have a few minutes, focus on the significant things. First try to figure out whether or not this person is suited for you. Within a couple of minutes you'll already be getting a certain feel from that person.

Whether it's a good thing or not, you have every bit of power to steer the date your course of direction, so to speak. You must emit a confident, driven and likeable energy. That way your date would feel more comfortable and conversations will by easy. It's also a practice of good judgment. Keeping an open mind is key.

Don't shut yourself to the idea of seeing this person until you get to know them. Zone in on what the person's life feels like, and whether or not he or she's happy with it. In the long run, the success or failure of the date will depend upon the little things that the other individual does or says -- just like in a conventional dating situation. The little things count.

The Basics

Everyone prepares for dates in their own special way; may it be an elaborate bath routine or stress-relieving yoga positions to achieve the best state you can for the dating game. However the magical structure of speed dating requires that you at least have an idea of your dating preferences. Before you go into the sitting, a good trick would be to formulate a simple list of all your likes and dislikes.

It will help cross out some of the other time consuming elements, as well narrow down all your thoughts so you wouldn't have to stammer out things you'll later on regret or feel stupid for. Be cool and keep it simple. Jot down personality quirks that irritate you and any likely "deal breakers" -- traits or habits that you'd never wish to find in an individual you date. If any of your speed dates exhibit these traits, then you are able to speedily eliminate them as feasible companions.

It likewise helps to compose a short mental list of favorable traits, too. Either things that you love, traits you'd like them to have, or things that you would like to undergo while dating. Remember, it never hurts to be a bit adventurous. And it's all in the fun of speed dating, so go on ahead! But keep in mind that all the rainbows and butterflies kick in during the relationship. Not within a couple minutes of googley-eyed gazes and "so tell me more about yourself" lines.

Here's how it goes: Interested men and women assemble at a preset spot. While the women sit at individual tables, the men go around in 10 minute intervals till they've met and talked to each woman in the room.

As the evening starts to wrap up the shindig, you let the event organizer know which individuals you're interested in seeing again, and the organizer gives out contact info.

What you choose to do next is totally up to you! Now ain't that fun?

During a speed dating event, too many individuals pretend to be somebody they're not in hopes of getting more individuals interested in them, as well as raking in a higher number of dates. This is a complete and total waste of time. The object of speed dating is to find a suitable and potential partner within 10 minutes of agonizing fun. 10 minutes to find someone and impress them with just you.

Not the shiny, fake image you want to portray but the person who's going to end up working hard for the relationship. The person who will either enjoy being in love or suffer with not only a broken heart, but an identity crisis now too! You owe it to yourself to be the best person you can be. So but your best face forward and love the skin that you're in.

Think about it this way: if you wish to find somebody to be with for the long run and go on romantic dates with, and share the kind of

loving you're dying to give, they have to like you for who you are. Communicate. Reach out to that person as who you are from the very beginning, the very first time you reach her table and the seconds start ticking. You won't only discover that person a whole lot better, but you might also discover the correct somebody. That person that could finally, maybe, be "The Right One." And that's a big thing!

The amusing thing about speed dating is that you only have six to ten minutes to decide who you view is dating material! Just a good-sized amount of time to dive into the sea of chance. So you might as well make the best of it and have a couple of solid questions organized.

It's likewise advantageous to have answers for these questions at the ready! Think about the most common sorts of questions you're more than likely to be asked and devise a short response for each.

There is nothing worse than bumbling for words in spot where you only have a few minutes to make that all-important initial impression. This is where I remind you that the little list we discussed earlier is key.

It's likewise a great idea to prepare a mini "Personal Infomercial" -

- A really short 1 to 2 minute life history about yourself that highlights a few favorable aspects of your personality. Have it memorized and ready to blurt at a seconds notice. Do keep it fun

and light! This isn't History class so easy on the walk down memory lane unless you want your date bored out of their minds.

Alright then! That sums it up. The following chapters will delve into the other topics you would like to be taught in, as well as some that you might not already know and very important instructions you need to follow.

Chapter 2:

Basic Grooming Tips

Synopsis

Basic grooming tips for both him and her.

Some Basics

For Him

A well-groomed man is not just appealing to women these days. In fact, being clean and well-groomed can give you that boost of self- confidence that will work magic on you and the people that are just waiting be charmed smitten by you. A clean-cut look can give you that extra lift; this wonderful feeling like you can take care of anything in your life. The confidence will just naturally flow. A well-groomed man is sexy. If you want to add that extra appeal in your personality, find out some men's grooming tips to help you start transforming yourself into someone more appealing to women. Ever heard of GQ?

The yellow brick road to a sexy new you, minus the dirty:

1. Always, always maintain a clean shave. Don't let your beard grow beyond being unattractive. No woman would want to snuggle up next to a hobo and kiss a network of facial hair. Learn how to give yourself a clean and smooth shave. Among the important things to keep in mind when shaving is to do so after showering, while the pores are still open. Or you can place a facecloth in warm water, place it on top of your beard area for 30 seconds and then shave. It is important to invest in a good quality razor and shaving cream. This will help you avoid having shaving bumps, annoying cuts and wounds that will end up as gross little patches of white on your face as you're walking down the street.

1. Maintain a good haircut, as well as clean hair all the time. Hair is a symbol of power. Of style. And so of

course the woman mind takes this into account as something that matters. A feat that is also one of the biggest deciding factors in attraction. Make sure you have no dandruff and your hair is neatly trimmed. Itchy white flakes are a big no-no. Also make sure that the hair style you're going to get is perfect for your face shape. Salons as well as barbers would know this as common knowledge. Before getting a haircut ask them first which hair style is best suited for your face shape. The result is a big high- five and a better looking you. Avoid using too much grease or oily hair product on your hair as it tends to give your hair a grimy look and feel. Less is more. Just a little product, along with the right shampoo and conditioner, can go a long way.

3. Free yourself from unpleasant odors. This may be one of the basic things to keep in mind not only for those who want to be well- groomed but for every man and woman out there. Deodorants, foot powder and mouthwash are among the things that may help you stay squeaky-clean and fresh. Making sure that your whole body is clean is also one of the basics when it comes to men's grooming tips to stay free from body odor. Scented body wash, as well as the right type of cologne and deodorant is key.

4. Observe proper body grooming. Although a little hair may be acceptable, you must know which is acceptable and which nasty, black curls must be kept away. Unkempt hair anywhere in the body that is not appealing, thus one of the men's grooming tips to keep in

mind is to invest in a good quality shaver or razor to trim those unwanted curls. Although hair in your armpit may be acceptable, trim them if they are way too think and unkempt. A little chest hair alright but please do shave once it starts to resemble a bush. Trimming and getting rid of messy pubic hair is also recommended. In fact, getting rid of the hair down there can help prevent odors within those areas, as the hair locks in all the sweat and odor. Here's another healthy reminder for all you fellas: Change your tidy-widies! If it ain't white, it ain't right.

5. Maintain clean fingernails and toenails. Dirty fingernails are always out when it comes to being attractive to women. Take time to clean your nails, a step that will always be in your best interest. Long, dirty sharp nails are so stone age. Have someone clean it for you or go to a salon for cleaning. It is common for men to even go as far as putting on some colorless nail polish to protect their fingernails. It is also quite endearing to women to think of men who take pride in presenting themselves as clean and well groomed.

These are the basic tips for Men's grooming. Stick to these and I assure you, you're going to be one hell of a catch!

For Her

When you're out with your girl friends, look at the way they're dressed and make a note of what you like about their sense of fashion, style and their trendy outfits. You'll probably notice things like their fabulous vintage Sixties shift dress, bold geometric earrings,

beautifully streaked urchin crop or elaborate eyeliner teamed with metallic eye shadow for a cutting-edge, feminine and glamorous look. It's always fun to experiment with all sorts of make-up and play up your wardrobe with unexpected twists in your closet expertise. But it's always good to stick to what you know; clothing that you're comfortable with and make-up that contours your face just right.

If, however, you ask a man to comment on your mates' attire, he'd probably point out 'the one in the shapeless dress, her with the big triangles in her ears, that one with short boy's hair and her mate with the scary gold eyes.'

Men see women's appearances in a very different way from other women. While ladies judge how a certain look works on someone, men are more likely to notice certain staples they find attractive or repellent, and ignore the rest. Be aware of the things guys always find it hard to stomach, as well as what will make you stand out in their eyes.

Too Much Make-Up

This doesn't just mean foundation so thick you could chuck rocks at it. Men aren't keen on very obvious make-up such as bright red lips or bold eye shadow. You could be wearing the most recent runway make-up looks and all they'd see is a blotchy face resembling some sort of wild tropical fruit. They prefer a bird's eye view into the canvass of a woman, which is her face. To be able to see what a girl's face looks like without a lot of paint on her skin. What you think looks

colorful, futuristic or vamped-up, they'll see as obscuring your features, somewhat unattractive, and ill-fitting. Keep it classy. Only lay on the make-up during night outs or photo opts. Invest in High Definition Make-up to prevent layering on the make-up too thick. With this tip all you really need is a few clean swipes. You'll be defined without having to be too overdone.

Come-Hither Eyes

Quiz any group of men on their favorite (non-sex-related) parts of a woman and the top response is bound to be 'nice eyes'. Make the most of the 'windows of your soul' by dolling them up with eyeliner, highlighter and mascara to emphasize, contour and reshape. This also opens up the area, making your most beautiful asses shine forward. Keep it clean and go easy on the rest of your face, keeping the blush and lipstick to a minimum so the immediate focus is on your eyes. That should give them plenty to gaze into longingly... Don't be afraid to dress up your peepers! But don't go crazy over them. Know when and where to use the appropriate amount/make-up look. Whether it's out and about town, or a hot night at a club, or a dainty wedding. You should always follow these codes, as well as remember: Make-up was made to enhance, not to make up for your whole entire face. Use meticulously. For more tips beauty salons and magazines can cater to all your beauty mishaps and teach you more on what you want to learn more about.

Over-sized Jewelry

While adorning yourself with bold plastic necklaces, dangling chandelier earrings or fake bling, don't think the fellas will love it as much as you do. Men get confused when you wear anything that doesn't appear to be in proportion with your body - they don't get oversized clothing, teased 'big' hair or six-inch platform heels either, because it doesn't fit the contours of your figure if you don't know which pieces compliment you best. And, of course, your figure's what they really want to be looking at. Invest in classic statement pieces that look good on you, as well as match your clothes and acts as a nice accent. Don't go overboard because that just screams tacky.

4. Stroke-able Hair

Gelled crops and tightly structured curls may be cutting-edge hair chic, but running your fingers through them isn't a pleasant experience. Men like long hair for a reason - it feels soft and silky in contact with their hands and skin. To get hair they're aching to touch, make sure your hair's clean, use an intensive moisturizing conditioner once a week to maintain body and don't use any harmful hair products that might damage your hair. Always consult an expert and resist the urge to do permanent make-overs at home. It will only spell out disaster. A safe trick would be a bottle of good ol' shine and or hair mist. But if you're a gal with limp hair and you're looking for that extra touch of vavavoom-volume, then go for a light weight volumizing formula. Great hair makes the fellas go wild.

Killer Heels

They look sexy, stated, sophisticated. The very definition of killer heels. But it's called 'killer' for a reason. It's hell on the soles! After a couple of hours, stilettos start to exert agonizing pressure on soles, pinch toes and blister heels, causing much hobbling and moaning about wishing you'd never worn them. Limping around in pain with blistered feet is not cute. Stick to comfier shapes if you know you'll be dancing. Also, a bit of height goes a long way. Grab a pair of shoes that look hot without having to hurt. Go for sense, before style. The pumps with padding are very merciful on your little piggies.

Knee-Length Boots

These are a winner on both fronts - women love them because they look stylish with everything from short skirts to jeans, while men adore the suggestive naughtiness of a long boot. Wear them with tights, though - bare legs and sticky leather don't go. A safe and sexy bet would be paring them off with your skinniest pair of jeans.

Loud Behavior

There's a world of difference between letting your hair down and dancing on the table after one too many shots of patron. Far from showing your playful side, such behavior is borderline rude. It will only intimidate and scare off men, since they prefer woman in more quiet, fun groups than the wild, loud ones. Most men prefer the sort of woman that doesn't seem likely to be able to drink them under the table, as well as the type that doesn't get carried out the bar for pesky

behavior. Know your limits and remember that public places aren't your personal playground.

Confidence

That one thing that could set you apart in a crowded room. The one thing everybody wants. The one that all our favorite style icons have in common is their ability to project an image of being entirely comfortable in their own skin. A big factor of our admiration towards them. Its undeniable attraction and swagger. It has to come off as natural. Don't try too hard because I assure you, you will make an ass out of yourself. If you look or behave as if you're trying to attract a man's attention, chances are you won't, because they don't want to be with somebody who spends their time putting on an act. Relax and take a breather and before you know it, there'll be dozens of men hoping you look their way. Roll your shoulders back; keep your chin up and your head held high. Nothing is sexier than confidence that can light up the whole room, or a person that could come off as so cool and yet down to earth. You'll be sure to garner a few double takes.

Chapter 3:

Where To Find Potential Partners

Synopsis

Ever wanted some hot stud or picture perfect arm candy? Hell yeah. Is it difficult? Not entirely so. Any teenager's tendency is crave for someone that's everything they've ever wanted.

They have this perfect picture in their head of what true love's supposed to be. Maybe that's why there are so many heartbreak songs on the radio. People get extremely anxious if they are about to date a person. And expectations, they'll just be the death of you.

Helping you find a great date is our motive. Here are some cool tips and ideas for your dating dilemmas!

Have A Look

Place

Visit popular places where you know a lot of different groups of people frequent. Be present in mind and in body. Try to mingle with them and start the conversation. Visit various places like clubs, parks, libraries and public functions where the vibe's all good and everyone's enjoying themselves.

Get to know them. You cannot judge a person by just having a look at them. That's a Mortal Sin in the rules of attraction. You can start a small conversation by saying "Hi". Keep is light and friendly. Don't force yourself onto them. If you're lucky, the conversation could stretch longer and you can have a shot at asking this person other more gutsy questions like family and friends. It gives them comfort to talk about such topics.

Ask them if they are interested in being friends. With so many social networking sites such as Facebook and twitter, keeping in touch is as easing as flying a kite. Don't hesitate to ask! A friend request can go a long way. Suppose they say yes in becoming friends with you, do not jump in joy. Try to be calm and cool and just ask them where you can meet them the next time. Acting like a 5 year old in iHop will start raising eyebrows. Be cool.

There is no such thing as being fashionably late. It's rude and it will lead to nothing but trouble! Avoid this by preparing everything you need for the date beforehand. Your outfit, cash, a present maybe. Give yourself the time needed to get ready and make sure you get there on the proper time. This is sure to get you points, plus, it's a very good practice.

Tips

If your object of affection is in the same class as you are, that's a bonus. Proximity is one of the best ways in getting to know someone better, as well as an element in attraction. Make her laugh or lend him a pencil. Get to know that person better. Hey! You can even suggest you two go on a study date!

After you guys start to get talking, try figuring out what that person's interests are. This is a good way to establish a good relationship with them, as well as get to know this person better.

If you're feeling confident, the next step would be asking them out on a date. But if you're not brave enough to label it as a date, try using the term "hang out" or maybe go together to a mutual friend's party. Either way they'll get the picture of you initiating a date, and the rest will fall in to place.

Make sure to make it worth the wait, time and effort! Don't let them go home feeling indifferent. Now is your chance to be with this person

and make them really, really happy. Therefore it is very important that both of you end the date with a big smile slapped on your faces...maybe even a lipstick mark on the cheek, if you're good.

Warning

If and when they reject you, don't sweat. That's just one person that passed on an opportunity to be with you. It is not a loss. Do not lose confidence. It might get you down, but don't let it keep you down. Stay strong willed and remind yourself that there is somebody out there who'd love to go out with you.

All set? We've covered the basics of confidence building. But keep going, because there's more. Read on, tiger!

Chapter 4:

Do's And Don'ts Of Dating

Synopsis

Love is in the air and the craving for a soul mate is just reaching newer heights. All the singles looking for love should get their dating basics right if they want their "soul mate" or destined other to be everything they dreamed they would and enter a beautiful new relationship.

Dating is your first introduction to your potential partner and it is also the first opportunity for you to introduce yourselves, aside from the pretty flirting. Dating helps you know if you and your date are compatible with each other.

Singles who are adventurous prefer dating through different ways like online dating, speed dating, blind dating, casual dating, serious dating and more aside from the usual help from family and friends. Online dating is the most preferred form of dating for many singles because of convenience and the increased selection pool.

What To Do

If you think you can jump at every opportunity with a positive outlook and the prepared mindset, you're wrong. The fact is that there are no fail-proof tricks or formulas for wooing the one you go on a date with. Sometimes couples just don't have the appropriate chemistry or life circumstances to accommodate each other. That being said, there are some key dating basics that must be kept in mind during your search for a partner.

While the internet is replete with rules on dating, there is always a dilemma on what to do and what not to do. This article presents some dos and don'ts that singles must adhere to if they want their dating to grow into a sweetened relationship. These dating dos and don'ts are just some observed rules of etiquette and behavior and do not give a one-size fits all guarantee. Different tricks work for different people as each one of us are different and are in different situations in life.

Do's:

- Look your best by dressing up appropriately for the even on hand. Never leave home looking like a complete mess. Always make a point to look your best.
- Always be on time.
- Compliment your date. Be sincere!
- If you are meeting for the first time or after online dating then meet in public and not in secluded pubs or bars.
- Be light-hearted and sober in your approach.

- Switch off your cell phone or turn it to silent mode before your conversation begins. Distractions signal a lack of interest and respect.
- If you are using online dating, make sure keep things moving quickly to keep interest up. You should answer messages within a day or two and plan to meet up, in person, after you have exchanged only a few messages. Having a pen pal is great but, if you build up too much rapport before meeting in person, things can become awkward when you don't have the space cushion of the internet between you two.
- Always exude a warm and positive energy. Laugh and the world laughs with you, cry and you cry all by yourself. Keep your date comfortable.
- Make eye contact with your date to show interest and respect.

- Ask questions. Get to know this person better, and keep the date going smoothly. Act interested.

Don'ts:

- If you are using online dating, share only the personal information you are comfortable with and NEVER share financial information or passwords. Don't forget that the internet is full as psychotic creeps, and you might have just sent a dirty message to a 70 year old sumo wrestler who has a thing for little boys.
- Do not drink too much during your date. In fact, keep drinking to a minimum, as nervous as you may be.

- Do not date a person who is otherwise involved seriously with someone else (couple, marriage, etc.)
- Do not go for sex on a first date. As exciting as it may be to hit a home run in the first inning, having or trying to get frisky on the first date almost always comes off in bad form.
- Do not lie to your date on any aspect of your life. Be your best self but be your true self.
- Do not reveal your inner most secrets or speak too much about yourself on the first meeting itself. Being honest and upfront is necessary, but there is a fine line between too much.
- Do not splash on too much perfume. No matter how attractive the smell is, too much is always a turn off. Keep it light. The fainter the scent, the more curious it and intrigued they will be to get close enough to get a whiff of you. Just give a sprit to key areas, such as the ankles and behind the knees, the wrists, and around the neck area.

- Do not be over critical about anyone or anything. Again, remain positive and keep composure.
- Don't pull dirty, political or religious issues, as tempting as it may be for some comic relief. These topics should be avoided for meetings where you are getting to know each other. They are highly controversial for most people and offensive too. Keep everything fun and steer away from the serious hot button topics for now.

Chapter 5:

The Art Of Seduction

Synopsis

To master the art of seduction is not rocket science or advanced algebra; anyone can achieve it if they are willing to spend the time and initiative needed to master it.

The art of seduction is all about creating a magic spell called attraction. The magnetic pull that's got you lusting and craving. Here's how it goes: To master the Art of Seduction you need to...

It's An Art

1. Create attraction. Before any seduction can take place, attraction must be present. There are many

things that will make a woman attracted to a man, such as confidence, humour, money; power...the list goes on. You must learn how to create attraction first before you can get down to it. Flirtation is a good one to start things off. Playing it cool and debonair works just as fine.

2. Start seducing. Once you feel that she is attracted to you, you can now move on to seducing her with your words and body language. Subtle things like lingering eye contact or the touch of a hand to her cheek can set rockets off flying into space. Use your sense of humour to make her laugh, and initiate as many slight body contacts as you can.

3. Express yourself with Body language. You will need to make her know that you are interested in her right from the beginning. Make constant eye contact with her, and lean your body towards her while you are talking to her. Once she realizes your intention and does not reject you, you can now move on to another level.

4. Bring her to a private location. By this time, you can already assess whether or not you have successfully seduced her. If she is willing to move to a private location with you, your chance of success is there. Be more physically close to her by touching and caressing her. Planting kisses here and there call for a trophy.

Follow this basic blueprint whenever you want to seduce a woman. Remember, to master the art of seduction, consistent practices need to be done. Do not give up when you are met with some rejections, just push on. Maybe you just aren't their cup of tea. And hey, maybe they aren't what you're looking for anyway.

Chapter 6:

Recovering From A Relationship

Synopsis

When a relationship comes to an end and two lovers have broken down to a mere part of each other's past, it's hard. From being together and in love to being alone and hurt, just friends if you're lucky.

It's going to take a lot to get back on your feet again, but this article will help. The process of recovering from a broken relationship is made up of 5 stages.

Each stage is vital if you wish to recover fully from your relationship. It might take several years or even longer, but recognizing these stages will help you recover from your loss more effectively.

Get Better

Acknowledgment
Here in this stage you finally come to terms with the end of your relationship. The break up is as real as the ground you walk on. You may feel hurt, helplessness and even

hatred. It is understandable. But unhealthy if you don't forgive later on. It is important at this stage to think things thoroughly and take things slowly and surely.

You might not be able to address them right away. So learn to focus on the happier side of life. Go shopping, check out a movie or hang out with your best buddies. Grill it into your head that you can survive a broken relationship. Sun shine is a surefire way to feeling a whole lot better. Go for a jog and get a work out from your heartache too! The reinvention process is a beautiful thing.

Let it Out

There is nothing healthy about keeping things bottled up. If you don't allow yourself to forgive and let go, you won't be able to move on from it. Do not let the bitterness consume you. Free yourself of the pain, grief and hurt. Don't let yourself lose control of the situation. Shed those tears and pour out your frustration. Express yourself by any means necessary in order to get those choking emotions out of your system. And then let go.

Nurture

You do not need to crawl under a rock and die. Allow people to help and support you during your recovery process. Spend time with people you care about. Do not run away from discussions about your broken relationship. Let them offer their opinions. However be cautious with the people you give this privilege, you don't want them adding to your pain and sorrows.

You can do without the anger and vengeance. You don't need it. Accept only positive feedback and encouraging words, good friends and great music and soul food. Order your favorite pizza and eat your heart out just because. Hold a sleepover or host a party to get yourself feeling a whole lot better.

Pamper Yourself

All the tears and late nights watching The Notebook and hate mail must end sometime. And now is finally the time to reward yourself. Don't seek revenge against your ex. Rather make yourself happy by working out, having your facials done or going shopping with the girls. Reward yourself in a healthy and positive way. Remind yourself that life does not end with a failed relationship and that you deserve better.

Learn and Move On

This is where you begin to see the bigger picture. Learning from the mistakes of the past and making the most out of the present so you can do your best in the future. Here you understand why the break up

occurred and what was responsible for the demise of the relationship. Now you can think back to all the times you two had before and not feel anything else but a fleeting sadness. You start thinking about the signs and something tells you that whatever happened, happened for a reason. And now you're finally happy again. By now, you are indifferent to your ex and would have totally moved on to happier times in your life.

Surviving a break up is never easy. But it is important that you acknowledge that the relationship is over and that all that's left for you to do is grieve a little. But Dr. Seuss wants us to remember to smile too, because it happened. And during that point in time you two were happy. Allow friends and family to nurture you. Remember to pamper yourself and learn from your mistakes and you will be just fine. It can't rain forever.

Wrapping Up

Now you've come to the final page of our adventure. I would just want to remind you to have fun, keep it real, and be the best you can possibly be. You won't always need to be dating or in a serious relationship throughout your whole life. But by the end of the day we all need that one person we can come home to.

I hope this will help you find the kind of love that keeps you warm at night. Thank you for letting me teach you everything I know, kid. And I wish you the best of luck! Don't forget; once the date's over go tell your best friend all about it! Listen to what they have to say and scream with them about how giddy the date made you feel.

<u>Keep it simple. Love simply.</u>

CHAPTER TWO

DEALING WITH LONELINESS

"An Open Invitation To Life, Love and True Companionship"

<u>LEGAL NOTICE</u>

The Publisher has strived to be as accurate and complete as possible in the creation of this report, notwithstanding the fact that he does not warrant or represent at any time that the contents within are accurate due to the rapidly changing nature of the Internet.

While all attempts have been made to verify information provided in this publication, the Publisher assumes no responsibility for errors, omissions, or contrary interpretation of the subject matter herein. Any perceived slights of specific persons, peoples, or organizations are unintentional.

In practical advice books, like anything else in life, there are no guarantees of income made. Readers are cautioned to reply on their own judgment about their individual circumstances to act accordingly.

This book is not intended for use as a source of legal, business, accounting or financial advice. All readers are advised to seek services of competent professionals in legal, business, accounting, and finance field.

You are encouraged to print this book for easy reading.

Dealing with Loneliness

TABLE OF CONTENTS

- 3

- 4 -

Dealing With Loneliness

"An Open Invitation to Life, Love and True Companionship"

Why I Wrote This Book

Welcome, my dear readers!

If you are feeling lonely as you are reading this, you are not alone. The reason why I put this book together is because I know what it is like. Loneliness is a topic that is very close to my heart because I have been through the depths of empty, meaningless feelings many times and I am not new to that kind of feeling.

I have felt every gripping moment of it. The long, long hours which seems like days, the lonely nights where I weep in silence, drenching my pillow salty with tears, the lack of desire to face the next day and the thought of wanting to *end it all*!

It doesn't matter if you have a girlfriend/boyfriend, husband or wife. No matter how close you are with them, there are parts of you that they just don't understand! The pain doesn't fade after confiding with your best friend, your group of buddies, or even your counselor! Nobody seems to understand you yet you want them to feel your pain.

I empathize with you, my friend. I truly do.

But I have good news for all of us lonely hearts out there. I have survived through and I have a way to solve it if not ease the pain at least.

My stories and writings in this book aim to accomplish a few things:

- Understanding the theory behind loneliness to better understand yourself
- Understanding the feelings associated with loneliness

- Developing a healthy feeling of love to help you overcome problems
- Practical steps to break the lonely cycle
- Replace the feeling of loneliness with healthy thoughts

It is my sincere wish that after you read this book, you will be better equipped to cope with loneliness. Even if you don't feel lonely, maybe you know someone who is. Use this information to help them and make their world a better place.

All Alone!

Everyone in the world has felt this emotion one time or another. Especially in these times rapid technological growth the feeling of loneliness is rapidly increasing.

Firstly, we must clarify what loneliness means.

Loneliness is an emotional state. This is a state where people experience a disconnection from people around them as well as a deep feeling of emptiness, which renders their present company around them meaningless.

That person could be in a big crowd or by him/herself, married or single, young or old. They basically find it very hard to connect with others and experiences emancipation from meaningful relationships.

This is not to be confused with being **alone**.

Being alone does not equate to being lonely because sometimes it is good for a person to be alone and at times it could be very refreshing as the person has the opportunity to refresh, recuperate and rediscover part of our lives.

What are the common symptoms of being alone, if you are reading this book? I bet you might be feeling one of these symptoms.

- You think your problems are so unique that other people do not understand
- As a result, you feel that other people in the world has friends and you don't
- You feel extremely self-conscious in everything you do
- You feel that when you do something wrong, you get extremely embarrassed
- When you are in a crowd, you feel drowned by their voices
- You feel disconnected with the crowd even though you are with them
- Feeling shy and scared of others
- Experiencing low self-esteem
- Feeling angry, defensive and critical at everything even if it is not directed at you
- Afraid of strangers and refuse to talk to engage in a hearty conversation
- Being convinced there is something wrong with you

- Feeling anxious and sad believing no one knows how miserable/isolated you feel
- Losing your capacity to be assertive' feeling "invisible"
- Refusing to accept change and don't want to try anything new
- Feeling as though nothing else matters and contemplating suicide

Crowded yet Isolated

Ever had that feeling that your wife or husband doesn't understand you? Your spouse or significant other is right beside you yet it doesn't fill that gap.

You may be surrounded by many people, yet their company 'drowns' you deeper into loneliness!

People feel that way because we are all unique and different. You see:

There is no one in the entire universe that will have the same personality, ideas, way of life and needs like you. NONE! Not even twins! How can anyone fulfill all those needs to cater every individual?

There us a quote from the bible that says if I try to remove the speck from my neighbor's eye, I must first remove the plank from my OWN eye then I can see clearly before I attempt to remove his speck.

How does this apply?

By understanding that other people are not obliged to fulfill our needs, we somehow learn to expect less from others and it eases the pain, because we stop expecting more from others! We learn to accept them better and judge others less so it creates the first step to curing loneliness – giving others slack!

Remember that we are the sum of the five people we spend most of our time with.

If you are mixing with a crowd that is negative and makes you feel down all the time, it is no surprise why you are lonely and negative. It is no surprise that children move out from their homes away from negative parents or stop interacting with certain groups of friends all together.

Don't let the poison drain your energy.

Emotional Pains in a loveless World

How does the agony of loneliness seem to penetrate the hearts of men and women throughout the world? Even superstars who have been the icon of generations and admired by millions feel unfulfilled (*e.g. Janis Joplin, Kurt Cobain*)

The feeling of loneliness is radically due to the failure of man in loving others. The symptoms of loneliness magnetize the effects of the pain to the extent that it forces the focus of attention more on ourselves and creates a self-preoccupation that creates an obstacle to love others.

Ever had a stomachache? Who are you thinking of at that moment?

This illustrates the point that we are only thinking of ourselves. It shows a terribly pain filled world in which we live in.

Furthermore, the pain does go away like a stomachache. The so called Mid-life crisis is turning more into a 'young adult' crisis now with suicide rates hitting the roof and most diseases in the world today mentally induced or cured in psychiatric wards.

The basis of trust between people is eroding and less and less people are opening up to one another. By failing to open up to others, the lonely symptoms spring up as other people will not open up to you if you do not open yourself to others first.

Love – The Verb, Not The Feeling

Love, or rather the lack of it constitutes the loneliness breeding in a person's heart. It is a scary fact to note that we are largely shaped by others (remember the sum of five people we spend most of our time with) who hold our destiny in THEIR hands.

We are what we are today – a product of those who loved us or have refused to love us.

Love gives life to others. But what is most important is to remember is that in order to love someone else effectively, we must love ourselves first! You can't give what you don't have!

You may think you 'love' a beautiful girl or a handsome guy if you don't love yourself (there is a song that goes: *I am nobody until I met you or my life is meaningless until you came into the picture) but that is not love.*

You may admire that person because he or she is good looking, you may worship that person because you think he or she is better, you may even sacrifice your life for him or her for your own selfish, self-gratifying ego, but you do not love.

Love is a verb. It is an action. The feeling of 'love' is actually a product of the verb or action. By loving yourself first, it forms the basis or foundation by which you love others without which it is merely a baseless act of self-deception that *appears* to be loving.

But how do we love ourselves if we have never been loved? In the next chapter we will explore this area.

Learning How to Love

How do I take the first step to deal with loneliness? By learning to love. But first we must examine the paradox to love.

When we are lonely, we feel like we are in an unbearable prison. By its very nature of loneliness is just like the stomach ache – the attention centers only on ourselves. So we try and fill this emptiness by finding others who will give us that very love we need.

People often try to do things for others to gain their love. They barter trade favors with each other thinking that they are loving people. We know that our loneliness can only be filled by the love of others and therefore we must feel loved by others.

The paradox of love is this:

If we seek to fill the void of our own loneliness in seeking love from others, we will inevitably find no consolation but only a deeper desolation. In other words, if we seek the love that we need, we will never find it.

When a person orients his life towards the satisfaction of his own needs, when he goes out to seek the love which he needs, he is basically self-centered, no matter how pitiful he is. As long as he focuses on himself, his ability to love will always remain stunted.

What is the solution then?

If a person seeks not to receive love, but rather to give it without strings attached, he will become lovable and he will most certainly be loved by others in the end.

We must stop being concerned with ourselves and begin to be concerned with others. Beginning with the end in mind – which focuses the results of the act of love others without concerned with self-gain, is the first step to gaining love and easing the pain of loneliness.

Every single person on earth has some capacity to love.

We all have some ability to focus the attention off ourselves to the needs and concern of others. It is the extent that we are willing to give, are we able to receive that amount of love from others.

Deciding to love others with no strings attached is like a donation (we don't expect anything in return, not even a satisfied ego or relieved guilt), not a barter trade. **When we ask others, "What have you done for me?" we have failed tolove.**

Even if at the beginning you are only able to love little, you will be loved little. That very love will empower you to grow and produce more love and in return receive greater love from others.

But always remember that in making this self-donation or self-sacrifice, our minds must always be focused away from ourselves or it wouldn't work.

The Laws of Attraction

As a man thinks, so is he.

Ever wonder why certain people get the polite, respectful, "*Good Morning, Sir*", and others get the, "*Hey Bud*" or "*Hey, Mac*" kind of treatment?

Think for a moment, now.

What is the difference between *Donald Trump* and a beggar besides a few billion dollars and a couple of skyscrapers?

The answer: The mushy inside your head.

You see, the way people react to you is due to the way you think about yourself. Why do you think people judge a book by its cover or a bad kind by the clothes he wears? I know it is unfair, but the way a person thinks in his heart, he will appear or even live out what he is thinking!

The Law of Attraction is not something new; it is the way things are. It is evident in Murphy's Law – the things we most don't want to happen to often happens to us, that is why a dropped buttered toast always land on the wrong side!

Even as a child in school, I have always hoped that when I saw sitting in class, and I didn't know how to answer a question the teacher asked, I always whispered in my heart, "*Don't pick me... PLEASE, don't pick me*" and the teacher always did. It didn't matter where I was sitting, the teacher had this mind reading ability that knew I didn't know the answer or wasn't paying attention.

How does this apply to overcoming loneliness?

If you 'project' an aura of unwantedness, you will feel unwanted and your friends will reject you unconsciously. Stop acting like a wet, unwanted puppy who just escaped from the pound.

Say to yourself, "*You find me attractive, loveable and good company.*" It is true we can't always convince ourselves that we are lovable, attractive and people love being around us.

But since we can't control what others think, this form of affirmation actually fools our mind into thinking WE ARE lovable and attractive.

Try it and see!

Practical Steps To Overcome Loneliness

There are a number of ways to begin dealing with loneliness that involve the need to develop friendships, doing things for yourself, or learning to feel better about yourself in general.

- **Constantly remind yourself that the feeling of loneliness is <u>TEMPORARY</u>**and you will get over it in time

- **Make an effort to talk to someone NEW**. I know it is hard, but you must develop momentum and the first step is usually the hardest but most necessary.

- **Put yourself in new situations where you will meet people**. Engage in activities in which you have genuine interest. Meet with people of similar interest

- Join societies like church groups, organizations and others

- **STOP listening to lonely songs** (*e.g. All by Myself – Celine Dion*)

- **OPEN yourself to others first**. Don't expect people to share their problems with a closed person

- **Don't judge new people on the basis of past relationships with old people**. Try to see each person you meet from a new perspective instead of bring judgmental.

- **Intimate friendships usually develop gradually as people learn to share their inner feelings.** Don't rush into intimate friendship by sharing too much or expecting that others will.

- **Don't just seek romantic relationships.** Platonic or even casual buddies can be extremely satisfactory.

- **Lead a well balanced life.** Never neglect good nutrition, exercise and sufficient sleep. One of the main causes of depression which leads to loneliness, is the lack of those things.

- **Spending time alone** will help you examine yourself more closely.

- **Don't be a parasite to your friends.** If you seek them for compassion and sympathy, they will be there for you. But if you repeatedly drone over and over about your problems, it becomes a nuisance and your friends will at best just entertain you.

- **Reflect back on good memories** and count your blessings.

- **Learn a new skill.** Success in achieving something will make you feel good about yourself.

- **If you are having long term depression, it is not wrong to seek MEDICAL advice.** It is perfectly normal to get a prescription because lack of certain chemicals in the body is also the source of depression and can be treated easily. If we feel hungry and seek food, having the right medicine in proper dosage is the right way to tackle depression and feel less lonely.

- **See a counselor** and talk in privacy.

- **Spend time in Prayer.**

Breaking the Destructive Cycle

A word of caution:

Don't act like a hero because you are lonely.

You may be surprised. Self-pity is a subtle form of pride. Proud people glory in their *achievements* while people who self-pity glory in their *sufferings*.

It is really dangerous to dwell too long in loneliness because we are created to have relationships with one another.

It is a strong part of human nature that cannot be erased. If you grew up living alone in a jungle, you will most probably interact with animals or plants and talk to them in your own language.

- The greatest worry is when someone dwells too long in their loneliness these few things can happen.

- The loneliness addict shun all attempts to reconnect rendering their people around them lots of pain when their efforts to help the person gets rejected.

- The relationships around them slowly crumbles and when people start to ignore the lonely person, they will feel more justified when they finally exclaim, "Look at them; I was right all along that they never cared for me at all!"

- The loneliness addict eventually gets immune to the pain and embraces loneliness as a way of life. He is too lazy to change.

His disease spread to other 'survivors'.

This should motivate you enough to take action. Don't wait, do it NOW!

Here is an interesting quote:

Loneliness was the first thing that God's eye named not good.

- John Milton

Finding Our Purpose in the Wilderness

Here is a story designed to motivate you. When the dust settles and we have made all the money in the world, reached the height of fame and obtained the epitome of power, what gives us true meaning in life?

Many living things need each other to survive. If you have ever seen a Colorado aspen tree, you may have noticed that it does not grow alone. Aspens are found in clusters, or groves.

The reason is that the aspen sends up new shoots from the roots. In a small grove, all of the trees may actually be connected by their roots!

Giant California redwood trees may tower 300 feet into the sky. It would seem that they would require extremely deep roots to anchor them against strong winds. But we're told that their roots are actually quite shallow -- in order to capture as much surface water as possible. And they spread in all directions, intertwining with other redwoods.

Locked together in this way, all the trees support each other in wind and storms. Like the aspen, they never stand-alone. They need one another to survive.

People, too, are connected by a system of roots. We are born to family and learn early to make friends. We are not meant to survive long without others.

And like the redwood, we need to hold one another up. When pounded by the sometimes vicious storms of life, we need others to support and sustain us.

Have you been going it alone? Maybe it's time to let someone else help hold you up for a while. Or perhaps someone needs to hang on to you.

--- **Author Unknown** ---

Life Still Has A Meaning

I will end this book with a poem. Read this s few times and let the meaning sink in.

If there is a future there is time for mending- Time to see your troubles coming to an ending.

Life is never hopeless however great your sorrow- If you're looking forward to a new tomorrow.

If there is time for wishing then there is time for hoping- When through doubt and darkness you are blindly groping.

Though the heart be heavy and hurt you may be feeling- If there is time for praying there is time for healing.

So if through your window there is a new day breaking- Thank God for the promise, though mind and soul be aching,

If with harvest over there is grain enough for gleaning- There is a new tomorrow and life still has meaning.

~ Author unknown~

Take care and have a wonderful life!